Rag Quilting for Beginners

❖ **Complete, Step-by-Step Photo Guide**

❖ **Three Fun, Easy Tutorials**

❖ **11 Rag Quilt Patterns**

By Felicity Walker

QuiltersDiary.com/ragquilts

COPYRIGHT © 2015 FELICITY WALKER
All rights reserved. All photos by Felicity Walker
or used by permission under a Creative Commons license.

ISBN: 1512013269
ISBN-13: 978-1512013269

Contents

CHAPTER		PAGE
1	The easy, cozy fun of making rag quilts	3
2	How rag quilts are different from other quilts	6
3	Tools and supplies	10
4	Design variations	12
5	Fabrics, cutting, quilting, and piecing	14
6	Finishing seams and edges	20
7	Project #1: Quick Strips Rag Quilt	24
8	Project #2: Classic Squares Rag Quilt	28
9	Project #3: Nine Triangle Rag Quilts in One	31
10	Learn more about quilting with Felicity Walker	45
	About Felicity	45
	Photo Credits	46

1/ The Easy, Cozy Fun of Making Rag Quilts

If you can cut a strip of fabric, sew a (reasonably) straight line on your sewing machine, and use a pair of scissors, congratulations! You have all the skills you need to be a rag quilter.

This book will introduce you to the fun of making rag quilts and guide you step by step through your first projects.

What's Special about Rag Quilts

Rag quilts are everyday quilts, casual quilts, snuggle-up quilts made to be *used*: dragged around, thrown in the wash when they get dirty, then fluffed up and used some more. You won't typically see rag quilts on display at quilt shows or in museums. But everybody who gets a chance to wrap up in a rag quilt loves that feeling of cozy softness.

I always keep one in my car for my teenagers huddle under on the way to school on cold days. We have a couple in our family room to snuggle up in while we watch TV.

Rag quilts make wonderful baby gifts. New parents love to wrap babies up in them after a bath or at nap time. I gave one to my new niece and get a thrill from seeing her with it in the photos her mom posts online.

One of the best things about making rag quilts is that they are just *so easy*. You make them using a fast and forgiving quilt-as-you go method that speeds up the process of making your quilt and helps hide any mistakes you might make. Need a last-minute gift? You can throw a rag quilt together in a day or less.

Another great thing about making rag quilts is all the things you *don't* have to do. You don't have to cut out hundreds of fussy little fabric pieces, sew your quilt together with operating–room precision, baste it with dozens of safety pins, wrestle the whole thing under the sewing machine for machine quilting, or sew together lots of fabric strips to make a quilt binding. Rag quilting is the easiest way to quilt that I know of.

You can use new fabric to make a rag quilt, or recycle old shirts, sheets, blue jeans, chenille bedspreads – pretty much any fabric that takes your fancy.

What's In This Book?

Everything you need to know to make your first rag quilts is here:

- A guide to the tools and supplies you'll need.

- Step-by-step photo instructions for choosing fabrics, cutting, layering, quilting, sewing your quilt together, and finishing the outer edges.

- Tutorials for three fun and easy rag quilt projects, with complete fabric requirements and cutting instructions.

- Patterns for eight more unique rag quilts you can make with the blocks from Project #3.

Ready? Let's get started!

As a first step, I'd like to invite you to join my mailing list. You can sign up here:

QuiltersDiary.com/ragquilts

I will send you a bonus rag quilt pattern just for signing up. You will also receive my free newsletter with tips on quilting techniques, tutorials for favorite quilt blocks, quilted holiday projects, and much more. I'm also available to answer quilting questions.

If you would like to know more about quilting basics, I recommend *Quilts for Beginners*, my best-selling book for new quilters. It's available in paperback and as an eBook on Amazon.com.

Thanks for reading, and happy quilting!

Felicity Walker

Project #1: Quick Strip Rag Quilt

This quilt was so easy that I made it from start to finish in one afternoon, without even breaking a sweat. The whole quilt has only seven seams in all. It's a ~~lazy~~ busy quilter's dream, the perfect first quilt to make if you're a new rag quilter. The quilt is just the right size to make as a baby or child gift, and the big open strips are perfectly suited to all the adorable fabrics available for children.

Project #2: Classic Squares Rag Quilt

You will see variations on this rag quilt in photos all over the Internet. This pattern is so popular because it's so simple. With the right fabric choices, it looks terrific too. The shabby chic version in this book uses three flannel fabrics. I give you complete cutting, sewing, and finishing instructions for making the quilt, plus advice on making it in different sizes.

Project #3: Nine Triangle Quilts in One

The half-square triangle block used in this easy star quilt is one of the essential blocks every quilter should know how to make. This project starts with a half-square triangle tutorial. Then you will learn how to assemble your triangle blocks into this beautiful and surprisingly simple quilt.

But that's just the beginning! This project also includes patterns for eight more completely different quilts you can make using exactly the same quilt blocks. The only thing you have to change is the way you lay out the blocks. How cool is that?

2/ How Rag Quilts are Different from Other Quilts

RAG QUILTS ARE different from standard quilts in several ways. This chapter covers the important differences and what they mean to you as a rag quilter.

Quilt-as-You-Go is the Rag Quilting Way

When you sew a rag quilt, you layer and quilt each block or section separately, before you sew any of the sections together. Working in smaller sections is called quilting as you go, and it is much easier than the standard method of making a quilt, which involves sewing together the whole quilt top first, then sandwiching and quilting the whole thing all at once.

Try quilting as you go, and I think you'll agree that it's much more fun to work with one block or one section at a time than it is to wrestle the bulk of a whole big quilt through the throat of your sewing machine.

Every Layer Shows on a Rag Quilt

When you make a standard quilt, you focus most of your effort on the quilt top, because that's the part of the quilt you see the most. The middle batting/wadding layer is buried between the top and backing layers and is never seen at all. The back side of the quilt is often hidden on a bed or against a wall.

Not so for a rag quilt. All three layers of the quilt show in the seam allowances between blocks and in the quilt's outer edges. This happens because of the way you sew a rag quilt, which I'll describe in detail in Chapter 5.

Take a look at the quilt below. You can see its white backing layers quite clearly in the seams between the blocks. With all the layers in plain view, you need to be especially aware of how the fabrics from the back layers will look on the front of the quilt.

Clipped Seams Instead of Sashing

Many standard quilts have narrow strips of fabric called sashing between the blocks. Sashing gives the quilt a regular structure and keeps busy blocks from looking *too* busy. Here's an example of a conventional quilt with gray sashing:

A rag quilt's fringed seams play the same role that sashing does in regular quilts: they separate and show off the different sections of your quilt. You can use the seam allowances to create interesting lines of color that run through your quilt. See how the rag seams outlining the squares in this denim rag look almost like sashing:

You can make your rag quilts look more interesting by using extra-wide seam allowances and choosing contrasting colors for the backing layers of your rag quilt.

Clipped Outer Edges Instead of Binding

Standard quilts have a continuous strip of fabric binding around their outer edges that protects the raw edge of the quilt sandwich and often adds a touch of visual contrast. The quilt on the right has typical strip binding around the outside.

Rag quilts don't usually have this kind of binding (although you *can* bind a rag quilt with strip binding, if that's what you like.) Instead, a typical rag quilt has fringed outer edges that act as visual "binding." Here's an example:

You create the fringes by snipping the quilt's outer edges with special clippers made just for rag quilting. Then you wash the quilt to fluff up the clipped sections. I will show you exactly how to do this in Chapter 6. It's a lot faster and easier than making standard quilt binding!

Different Layers than Standard Quilts

All quilts are made in layers. The typical quilt consists of three layers:

1. Quilter's cotton on top
2. Batting/wadding in the middle
3. Quilter's cotton again on the bottom.

The layers in a rag quilt are a bit different:.

1. Top layer: flannel, quilter's cotton, or recycled fabric

Flannel is everyone's favorite rag quilt fabric. You can use it for all three layers of a rag quilt.

Quilter's cotton. I like to use this the top layer of my rag quilts because I have so much of it, and because it comes in so many wonderful colors and prints. It works just fine as a rag quilt's top layer, but isn't soft enough for the bottom layer that touches the skin, though.

Recycled fabrics. Many quilters like to make the top layer of a rag quilt from old shirts, bed sheets, worn blue jeans, even old towels and chenille bedspreads. I love this quilt made from plaid shirt fabric:

The floral fabric I used for Project #3 in this book (p. 31) started out as a sheet I was given by a relative. The sheet didn't match any of my other linens, but it was too pretty to give away. What to do with it? I cut it up and made it into a rag quilt.

2. Middle layer (optional): flannel instead of quilt batting/wadding

A middle layer isn't required for a rag quilt. If you want to make a lightweight quilt for a new baby or a quilt to be used in a hot climate, it's perfectly fine to leave out the middle layer altogether and just make a two-layer quilt with top and backing layers.

Conventional quilts use batting (also called wadding) as their middle layer. You *can* do this in a rag quilt, but I don't recommend it. There are two reasons why:

- **Durability.** In most quilts, the batting never sees the light of day. It is completely encased between the quilt's top and bottom fabric layers. Because of this, commercial batting isn't designed to handle the kind of wear an outer layer gets. If you handle some batting, you will feel how soft and unfinished it is. Since the middle layer of the rag quilt is exposed to wear, batting might not be the best choice.

- **Color choices.** Commercial batting comes in a very limited set of colors (usually beige or white, and sometimes black.). Using batting limits the color choices you have in making the quilt. I like to make my middle and backing layers from bright colors that make a strong color statement on the front of my quilt.

3. Bottom layer: flannel, Minky, or polyester fleece

The bottom layer of the quilt is the one that comes into closest contact with your skin, so you'll want to use the softest fabrics for it.

Flannel's softness makes it a wonderful choice for the bottom layer of the quilt. However, it's heavy, not terribly warm, and needs to be prewashed to minimize shrinkage.

I live in a cool climate, and so do most of the people I make quilts for. If that is your situation, you may want to try what I usually do: making a two-layer rag quilt sandwich that has a warm fabric like Minky or polyester fleece as its bottom layer.

Minky is a knitted polyester fabric with a super-soft furry finish. It is extremely soft, which makes it popular for baby quilts. It comes in a limited set of prints compared to polyester fleece, and it is usually more expensive than fleece. Minky is machine washable.

One warning about Minky: when you cut it, you may find your sewing room liberally covered with little snippets of Minky fur. (Don't ask me how I know this.) Just be ready with a vacuum cleaner!

Here's a piece of Minky with a bobbled finish:

Polyester fleece is my favorite backing fabric. It is very warm, lightweight, plush and soft. It comes in hundreds of different colors and prints. It cuts easily and doesn't fray or scatter little fibers all around your sewing room, but it does stretch and can get pulled out of shape. Fleece is very durable and can be machine washed and dried. It regularly goes on sale for half price at the big box fabric stores, so I buy in bulk when it is on sale and use up my stash between sales.

Here is a typical polyester fleece print:

If you are making a quilt for someone who loves a commercial character like Sponge Bob or Hello Kitty, you can probably find a fleece print at a big box fabric store that features the character.

Special Fabric Handling Requirements

Both Minky and polyester fleece have a tendency to stretch. That means you need to handle them with care to keep them from getting pulled out of shape, especially while you sew. If you have a walking foot, use it!

Flannel tends to shrink a LOT when it is washed and dried. I prewash my flannel at least once before quilting with it. Prewashing twice is worth considering, especially if your quilt combines flannel with a fabric that doesn't shrink.

3/ Tools and Supplies

MOST OF THE equipment and supplies you use to make a rag quilt are the same ones you need to make a regular quilt. This section covers the essentials you will need.

Rotary cutter. A cutter with a larger 60 mm blade is ideal for rag quilting, because you may be cutting through quite a few layers of fabric in the later stages of trimming and squaring up your quilt. Cutting through thick layers is easier with a larger blade.

Don't worry if your rotary cutter isn't 60 mm, though. I use my trusty old 45 mm cutter for rag quilts and everything else. Sometimes I have to make a couple of extra passes with the cutter to get through all the layers, but the quilt still gets cut in the end.

See-through cutting ruler. If you don't already have one, I recommend a 6" x 24" ruler with a no-slip back.

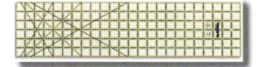

Cutting mat. You will need a self-healing mat designed for rotary cutting.

Basting spray. This helps you stick the layers of your quilt together temporarily until you can stitch them together permanently. I use 505 Spray and Fix Temporary Fabric Adhesive from Odif USA for basting. If you really don't like using spray, you can use large safety pins instead.

Sewing machine. Any machine that sews a good straight stitch is just fine for making rag quilts.

Walking foot. You will be sewing through several layers when you sew quilt sections together, so a walking foot or some kind of automatic fabric feed device is a huge help in keeping the top and bottom layers from shifting while you sew. The walking foot helps feed the fabric layers under the needle at the same rate while you sew. The thicker the layers are, the more a walking foot will help. If your sewing machine doesn't have a feeding device or walking foot built in, you can get a separate walking foot that mounts on your sewing machine.

Here is what a typical walking foot looks like:

All-purpose or quilting thread in a color that coordinates with your fabrics. I use 40-weight polyester quilting threads from YLI or Superior Threads. Some people prefer cotton thread. There are many good thread brands out there. If you don't already have a favorite brand, your local quilt shop can recommend one.

Iron to press your fabric and keep it smooth and unwrinkled while you work on your quilts.

Rag quilt snips for fringing the seam allowances. You may be tempted to use scissors to clip your seam allowances, but rag quilts make the job much easier and faster. They are less fatiguing to your hands than regular scissors.

If you must use regular scissors (not recommended, because of the strain on your hands), use a spring-loaded type like these from Fiskars. The spring helps do some of the work of snipping for you, but rag snips have a stronger spring that does much more of the work and reduces the strain on your hands.

Of course I like rag quilts. Don't you?

4/ Design Variations

THE CLASSIC RAG quilt has ragged edges around every single piece of fabric. The quilt shown below is an example of this style:

That's not the only way to make a rag quilt, though. You can create a number of different looks in your quilts by combining traditional piecing with rag piecing. Here are two ways of making a rag quilt that can give your quilt more visual interest.

Traditionally Pieced Blocks with Rag Seams

After I made a few rag quilts with basic square blocks, I started wishing for a design with a little more visual pizzazz. It dawned on me that I could take a simple quilt block like a Four-Patch or Half-square Triangle and make a rag quilt out of that.

The photo below shows a section of the first half-square triangle rag quilt I made. I pieced the triangle blocks with standard quilting seams and 1/4" seam allowances. When I assembled the blocks into a quilt, I sewed the blocks together with rag seams and 3/4" seam allowances. You can make lots of different blocks into rag quilt blocks in just the same way.

If you use this approach, remember that the seam allowances around the outer edges of the blocks will be wider than they are in a normal quilt. This means that a 3/4" strip around the outer edges of the block will be used up by the extra-wide seam allowances when you sew the blocks together. That's why I chose a simple, symmetrical block for this technique. Stealing an extra slice of the blocks didn't change the proportions of the block. This isn't true of every quilt block. On a Log Cabin block, for instance, which is made from strips built around a center square, the seam allowances could cut off most of the outer strips and leave you with an awkward-looking block.

Traditionally Pieced Center with Rag Borders

Another way to give your rag quilt a different look is to piece the center of the quilt the standard way, then add the borders using rag seams. That's how I made the quilt below. I pieced the whole center section with standard quarter-inch quilter's seams. Then I layered the pieced section with middle-layer and backing fabrics and machine quilted the whole center section.

After that, I cut and machine quilted each border section of the quilt as a separate unit. Finally, I sewed the borders to the center section of the quilt with rag seams.

This is one of my favorite ways to make a rag quilt. It's a more finished look than the most basic rag quilt designs, but it is still very easy to sew. You just have to keep in mind that the larger you make the center section, the bulkier it is, and the harder machine quilting it becomes. When it comes to quilting, small sections are always easier to handle than large ones. So think small when you plan your rag quilts.

5/ Fabrics, Cutting, Quilting, and Piecing

This chapter guides you step by step through the first parts of making a rag quilt. Chapter 6 covers the finishing steps.

1. Choose the Fabrics

Like any quilt, a rag quilt is all about the fabrics. I could write a whole dissertation on the mysteries of fabric colors and how various colors work together, but you can make wonderful quilts by following just a few basic tips for fabric and color selection.

Top Layer Fabrics. I like to start by choosing a focus fabric that sets the mood and color scheme for the whole quilt. Then I study the focus fabric to choose colors and prints for all the other fabrics in the quilt. Don't be afraid to use a secondary color you like even if there's only a tiny bit of it in the focus fabric. Sometimes those minor colors really bring a quilt to life. Here's the assortment of fabrics I chose for a rag quilt for a baby girl. The owl fabric was the focus fabric:

Using a mixture of lighter and darker colors makes for a pleasing quilt. So does mixing smaller prints with larger-scale ones, or mixing contrasting patterns like polka dots with stripes (within reason!).

Middle and Backing Fabrics. Once you have settled on your top layer fabrics, choose fabrics with coordinating colors for the quilt's middle and backing layers. Remember that all three layers show on the front of the quilt. See how the pink-and-orange polyester backing livens up this Quick Strip rag quilt:

Have Fun! Probably the best advice I can give you on fabric selection is to follow your color instincts and choose colors and prints that make you feel good. If you don't trust your own sense of color, try looking at quilts on Pinterest.com or Flickr.com. Use the fabric combinations you like best as a starting point for choosing your own fabrics. I have two Pinterest boards for quilters, each with dozens of photos of gorgeous quilts that will get you started. You can find them at Pinterest.com/FelicityWBooks.

2. Cut the Fabrics

Cut the top, middle, and backing layers into identical-sized pieces. For instance: if the top layer of your quilt pattern consists of sixteen 10-inch squares, you will also need sixteen 10-inch squares of middle fabric and backing fabric. Here are the pieces I cut for the Classic Squares quilt in Project #2 (p. 28):

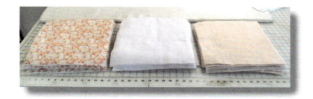

3. Layer the Blocks

This step calls for basting spray, so start by protecting your work surface from overspray by covering it with a piece of old fabric you can toss in the wash or some newspaper that can go in the trash afterwards. I cover my cutting table with a flat bed sheet. Also make sure that the room you are working in is well ventilated.

If you can't use basting spray for whatever reason, you can use a couple of safety pins or even straight pins to secure the layers together instead.

Here's how to put your layers together:

- Lay a piece of the backing fabric on the work surface with its right side down. (For most fabrics, it's easy to tell which side is the right side.) Spray lightly with basting spray. Use a delicate touch with the spray. I try to hit the corners and edges with just enough to keep the layers from shifting.

- If your quilt has a middle layer, lay a middle layer square, right side up, on top of the backing fabric. Smooth out any wrinkles. If the wrinkles won't smooth away, lift up the top layer and reposition it. Once you have the fabric where you want it, spray this layer lightly with basting spray.

- Finally, lay a piece of the top fabric on top of the stack, right side up. Smooth away wrinkles.

Here is a block with the three layers in place:

4. Machine Quilt the Blocks

The next step is to stitch all the layers together. Rag quilts don't need a lot of quilting, but you should secure the layers with at least one or two seams so the quilt holds together when you use and wash it. I often quilt square rag blocks by simply sewing an X across them, like this:

If the block has seams in it, you can stitch along one or two of the seam lines to secure the layers.

A rag quilt block is a good place to practice new machine quilting motifs you'd like to try. How about practicing your stipple?

If you prefer, you can do fancier stitching. I stitched this free-motion leaf design onto some half-square triangle blocks:

Remember that any quilting you do right near the edges of the block won't show, because it will be part of the 3/4" seam allowance that runs all around the block. I like to quilt right up close to the edges anyway, because the quilting helps stabilize the edges of each block. That way, you won't get any puckers or stretching when you sew the blocks together.

5. Square Up the Pieces

Once you finish quilting, use a ruler and your rotary cutter to square up the corners and edges of your blocks or sections. This is especially important if you are using fleece, which has a definite tendency to stretch out of shape. Squared-up pieces align better with the other pieces when you sew the quilt together. Here's what to do:

- Put the corner of a cutting ruler over the block, aligning the corner of the ruler with one corner of the block.

- Trim off any extra bits that stick out from under the ruler, like the circled area on the photo below. Repeat on all corners of the block.

6. Sew the Quilt Together

Arrange the blocks on your design wall or work table into a pattern you like. Then sew the blocks together, one row at a time. I start at the upper left corner of the quilt and mark the top left block with a safety pin so I don't lose my place later.

- Align two blocks with their back sides together, as shown in the photo below. Pin the blocks in position if you want to (I usually don't.)

Put wrong sides together

- Sew the blocks together with a ¾" seam allowance. Some rag quilters use a ½" seam allowance, but I like the really fluffy seam lines you get with wider seam allowances. You can try them both and see which one you like best.

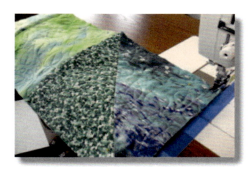

Note the piece of blue painters tape that marks the seam allowance on my sewing machine's bed. This is a great way to help keep your seams straight.

- Check after sewing to make sure the raw seam edges are on the TOP of the quilt, not the back side.

When you have all the individual rows assembled, sew the rows together, working from the top of the quilt to the bottom.

- Lay two rows together with their back sides facing each other. I do pin the rows together at this stage to make sure the seams between blocks are aligned with each other.

- Sew the rows together with a ¾" seam allowance.

With so many layers to sew through, the seams will be quite bulky at this point. You may have to manhandle them under the needle. If your machine refuses to sew through a thick area, you can rotate the fly wheel toward you and stitch through the problem area manually, one stitch at a time. This can save you broken thread or a broken needle.

When all the rows have been joined into a single unit, they should look something like this:

6. (Optional) Add Borders

Borders are a great way to enlarge a quilt that is too small or to create a visual contrast to the central part of your quilt. With rag quilts, you quilt and assemble the whole center section of the quilt before you add the borders. Then, each border is layered and quilted individually before you sew it onto the center section of the quilt. Here's how to add a simple border:

- First, square up the center section using the same method you used to square up individual blocks.

- Once the center is squared up, measure the height of the center section, as shown below.

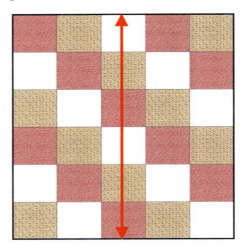

- Write down the measurement. This tells you how long to cut your side borders. For example, if the center section of the quilt is 40" high, your border strips need to be 40" long.

- Decide how wide you want each side border to be, then add 1½" to the width to account for seam allowances. If your quilt is 40" high and you want to add a 5"-wide border on each side, you will need to cut two fabric strips 40" long by 6.5" wide (5" + 1½" seam allowances.)

- Cut two identical-sized side border pieces from the middle layer fabric, and two more from the backing layer fabric.

- Layer the border fabrics the same way you layered the quilt blocks.

- Quilt each border individually.

- Sew the borders to the center section, using a 3/4" seam.

- Measure the width of the quilt with the side borders on. This measurement tells you how long to cut your top and bottom border strips.

- Decide how wide you want the top and bottom borders to be, adding 1½" to the width to account for seam allowances.

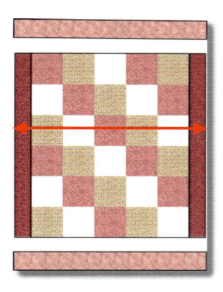

- Cut two identical strips of top layer fabric, one for the top border and one for the bottom border. Cut matching pieces of the middle and backing layer fabrics.

- Layer and quilt each border.

- Sew the top and bottom borders to the body of the quilt.

- Square up the quilt again.

You're almost done! In the next chapter, I'll show you how to finish the seams and edges.

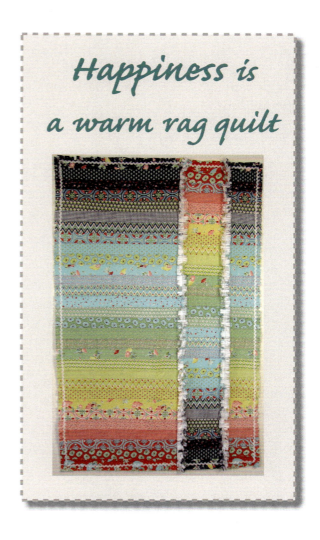

6/ Finishing Seams and Edges

ONCE YOU HAVE your quilt sections sewed together, you're in the home stretch. This chapter covers the final steps in finishing your quilt.

Clipping the Seams

I clip the the seam allowances between blocks and sections before I deal with the quilt's outer edges. Here's what to do:

- Hold the seam allowance in one hand to press all the layers together. Then use your rag snips to clip short cuts along all the seam allowances. Make the cuts perpendicular to the seams, like this:

- As you snip, place the cuts as close together as you can. The closer you make them, the fluffier the seams will look. Try to keep your cuts short enough that you don't cut through the seam line. But if you do do cut a seam, don't worry — it happens to all of us. Just take the quilt back to your sewing machine and re-sew that spot, backstitching at the beginning and end of the seam to secure your stitches.

Finishing the Outer Edges

One of the things I love about rag quilts is that they don't need any binding.

You *can* bind a rag quilt the same way you would bind any other quilt, by sewing a long, folded strip of binding fabric to the quilt's outer edge. Since that isn't strictly a rag quilting technique, I won't cover how to do it here. If you want to know how to make standard quilt binding and sew it onto a quilt, my book, *Quilts for Beginners #1*, has complete step-by-step instructions.

The two finishing methods shown here both give your quilt a distinctive raggedy edge—and they're both easier and faster than putting on standard quilt binding.

Method #1: Simple Clipped Edges

The easiest way to finish a rag quilt is to clip the outer edges of the quilt in exactly the same way you clip the seams between blocks.

- Before you clip, stay-stitch a seam all around the quilt's outer edge to keep the snipped edges from unraveling into the quilt later:

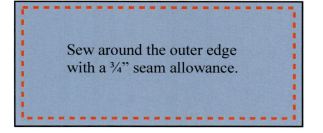

Sew around the outer edge with a ¾" seam allowance.

- Clip all around the outer edges of the quilt with your rag snips, exactly the same way you did for the inside seams. Take care not to cut through your stay stitching.

The photo below shows how a simple clipped edge looks. The technique is easy, but those outer edges look a bit skimpy to me. That's why I now finish almost all of my rag quilts with the second technique, which takes a *little* bit more effort.

Method #2: Edges Enhanced with Fabric Strips

This method gives your quilt a richer look around the outer edges, and it is still very easy! The photo below shows one corner of a quilt where I used the fabric strip finishing technique. The blue triangle is the outer corner of the quilt. It looks much plusher and more finished to me than a simple clipped edge.

To make this kind of edge, you need 1½" strips of two fabrics that coordinate with the colors of your quilt.

You will need enough strips of each fabric to go all the way around the outer edge of the quilt. The patterns in this book tell you exactly how many strips to cut, but if you want to design your own quilts, you may want to figure out how many strips to cut for yourself.

Here's how to do it:

*(Quilt length + Quilt width) × 2 =
Total inches of strips needed for each fabric*

Once you know how many inches of edge strips you need, you can calculate how many strips to cut. Assuming your fabric has 40 usable inches between its selvage edges, use this calculation to figure out how many strips of each fabric you need:

Total strip length / 40 = Number of strips to cut

Round up to the nearest whole number.

After you cut the edge strips, here's what to do:

- Starting at one corner of the quilt, lay strips of one fabric along the quilt edge. I've tried putting them right side up and right side down. Either way works. You can use a touch of basting spray to help keep the fabric in place, but I don't usually bother.

- When you come to a seam between blocks, open the seam allowances so they lie flat on the quilt top, then lay the edging strips over the seam allowances. Pin to keep the seam allowances flat, as shown in the photo on the left.

- When you reach the end of one strip, just lay down the next one so the ends touch or slightly overlap. If the strip is too long, trim it to length with a pair of scissors.

- Lay the second set of fabric strips on top of the first strips, with their right sides up. Pin as needed to keep the fabrics where you want them.

- After you finish laying the strips along one edge of the quilt, sew the strips onto the quilt, using a 3/4" seam. You will be sewing right down the middle of the strips, like this:

- Once you have sewed edging strips all around the quilt, clip the outer edge of the quilt and both sides of the edging strips with your rag snips. The cut strips should look something like this:

Finishing the Quilt

- After you clip all the seams, take the quilt outside and give it a good shake to get rid of as many of the little threads as possible before you wash the quilt. There will be a lot of little threads!

- Wash the quilt in your washing machine on the shortest possible cycle, using a minimal amount of detergent to wash away the basting spray. Some people prefer to use Woolite or Orvus, which are gentler than regular detergents. I use a small amount of my regular laundry detergent.

- Dry the quilt in the dryer.

Rag quilts produce a *LOT* of lint the first couple of times you wash them. If you are concerned about all that lint going into your plumbing, you may want to wash the quilt at a laundromat.

Our lives are like rag quilts – bits and pieces, joy and sorrow, stitched with love.

7/ Project #1: Quick Strips Rag Quilt (40" x 50")

FABRIC REQUIREMENTS

- Focus fabric: ¾ yard

- 3 color-coordinating fabrics for quilt body: 3/8 yard of each

- Middle layer fabric: 1-7/8 yard

- Backing fabric:: 1-7/8 yard

- Outer edge trim: ¼ yard each of two different fabrics, or ½ yard of one fabric.

If you have never made a rag quilt before, or even if you have never made a quilt at all, this little quilt is the perfect place to get started.

It is easy to cut, easy to sew, and very forgiving of any mistakes you might make. You can throw one together in less than a day, even if you are a complete beginner.

The instructions for this project go quickly through techniques that are covered in detail in Chapters 5 and 6. Please check back if you need a refresher.

1. Choose the Fabrics

Start by picking a focus fabric for the quilt. The focus fabric will be used for the largest strips in the quilt, so don't feel shy about picking bold colors or a large-scale print. I chose a cute animal print for my focus fabric. You can see it in the photo on the left.

Once you have the focus fabric, take a close look at its colors and its pattern and use them to help pick your coordinating fabrics. Here are the top layer fabrics I chose for this quilt:

I omitted the middle layer on this quilt and used a light gray polyester fleece for the backing fabric. You can see the lines of gray in the photo on the left.

2. Cut the Strips

This quilt is made entirely from fabric strips. Cut all the following strips the full width of the fabric.

Top Layer

- Focus fabric: Two 11½" strips
- Coordinating fabric 1: Two 6½" strips
- Coordinating Fabric 2: Two 6½" strips
- Coordinating Fabric 3: Two 4½" strips
- Edge trim fabrics 1 and 2: Five 1½" strips of each fabric. You could also choose one edge trim fabric and cut 10 strips instead of five.

Middle Layer

- Two 11½" strips
- Four 6½" strips
- Two 4½" strips

Bottom Layer

- Two 11½" strips
- Four 6½" strips
- Two 4½" strips

3. Layer the Strips

Make a set of top fabric, middle fabric, and backing fabric layers for each strip. Here's how:

- Lay the backing fabric strip on your work surface, right side down.

- Lay the middle fabric on top of the backing fabric, right side up.

- Lay the top fabric strip on top, right side up. Align the corners to make sure the layers are all straight.

4. Quilt the Strips

Machine quilting this quilt couldn't be easier: you simply sew seams down the strips from top to bottom. I used a wavy stitch from my sewing machine's library of decorative stitches, but a straight seam will look just as good. The number of seams you need depends on the width of the strip. Here's what I recommend for this quilt:

- 4-1/2" strips: sew one seam down the center of the strip.

- 6-1/2" strips: sew two seams that divide the strip into three equal sections.

- 11-1/2" strips: sew three seams. Sew one seam down the center of the strip, then one down the center of each side.

5. Sew the Sections Together

Lay the quilted strips on your work surface so they are arranged the way you want them to look when the quilt is finished. The photo below shows how I laid out my quilt:

Sew the strips together with a 3/4" seam, starting from the top of the quilt and working down to the bottom.

6. Add the Edge Trim Strips

Lay the two layers of trim strips around the outer edges of the quilt and sew them on.

7. Clip the Seams and Edges

Using your rag snippers or spring-loaded scissors, clip all the seams between strips and all around the outside edges of the quilt. Clip both sides of the edge trim strips.

8. Wash and Dry the Quilt

Shake off as much lint as possible outside, then run the quilt through the washer and dryer.

9. Make Another One!

The photo below shows the first Quick Strips quilt I made. I've made several more since then. This pattern has become my go-to quilt whenever I need to make a quick gift.

Making a strip quilt is a great way to try out new fabric combinations. You can also vary the width of your strips or the number of fabrics you include in the quilt. Use this easy pattern as a springboard for your adventures in creative quilting.

8/ Project #2: Classic Squares Rag Quilt (45" x 55")

FABRIC REQUIREMENTS

- White flannel: 4-5/8 yard
- Pink rose flannel: 1-3/8 yard
- Pink chevron flannel: 1-3/8 yard
- Edge Trim: ¼ yard each of two different fabrics, or ½ yard of one fabric.

THIS PLUSH, COZY flannel rag quilt is just what you need when you crave a little extra softness in your life.

The instructions for this project summarize techniques that are covered in detail in Chapters 5 and 6. Turn back to those chapters if you need a refresher.

1. Choose the Fabrics

This quilt has just three fabrics. I went for a soft, cottage chic look by choosing solid white and two pale pink prints for the top layer, then white flannel as the middle and backing layers. Here are the fabrics I chose:

2. Cut the Fabric

This quilt is made entirely from square blocks. Every square in the quilt is exactly the same size. That makes the cutting simple! Cut the following pieces:

Top Layer

- Ten 10" white flannel squares
- Ten 10" rose flannel squares
- Ten 10" pink chevron flannel squares

Middle Layer

- Thirty 10" white flannel squares

Bottom Layer

- Thirty 10' white flannel squares

Edge Trim Strips

- Twelve 1½"white flannel strips the full width of the fabric.

3. Layer the Squares

Make a set of top fabric, middle fabric, and backing fabric for each square:.

- Lay the backing fabric square on your work surface with its right side facing down.
- Lay the middle fabric on top of the backing fabric, right side up.
- Lay the top fabric strip on top, right side up.

Align the corners to make sure the layers are all straight.

4. Quilt the Squares

My favorite way to quilt simple squares like these is to just stitch an X across each square. See page 16 for a photo showing exactly how to place the X, plus some alternate ways to quilt the squares.

You can mark a stitching guide for your X lines with a ruler and a wash-away pen, but I find it's more fun to just eyeball my seams. The end result looks fine.

5. Lay Out and Sew the Squares

- Lay the squares on your work surface so they are arranged the way you want them to look when the quilt is finished. Check your layout against the diagram below:

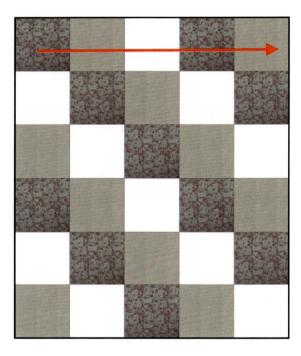

- It's easy to get disoriented when you're working with a lot of identical squares. I always put a safety pin in the square on the top left corner to help me keep my bearings while I sew.

- Sew the squares together, one row at a time. I sew each row from left to right, starting with the top row, then working my way down to the bottom of the quilt, one row at a time.

- Sew the rows together. Pin at seam lines to make sure the rows don't get out of alignment while you sew.

6. Add the Edge Trim Strips

Lay two layers of trim strips around the outer edges of the quilt and sew them on.

7. Clip the Seams and Edges

Using your rag snippers or spring-loaded scissors, clip all the seams between the squares and all around the outside of the quilt. Clip both sides of the trim strips.

8. Wash and Dry the Quilt

Run the quilt through the washer and dryer to fluff up the clipped seams, wash off the basting spray, and get rid of the lint that comes from all those clipped edges.

9. Making this Quilt in Different Sizes

Since all the pieces in this quilt are exactly the same size, it's easy to make the quilt larger or smaller. All you have to do is cut larger or smaller squares. The list below shows how big the quilt will be if you make it with different size blocks. The quilt dimensions are rounded to whole numbers.

- 9" blocks: quilt measures 41" x 49"

- 10" blocks: quilt measures 45" x 55".

- 11" blocks: quilt measures 50" x 61"

- 12" blocks: quilt measures 55" x 67"

If you change the size of the quilt, remember that you will need to adjust your fabric requirements. You will also need a different number of edge trim strips to go around the outer edges.

9/ Project #3: Nine Triangle Quilts in One (44" x 44")

FABRIC REQUIREMENTS

- Top Layer:

    –White fabric: 1-5/8 yards

    –Floral fabric: 1-5/8 yards

- Middle Layer: 3-¼ yards

- Backing Layer: 3-¼ yards

- Edge Trim: ¼ yard each of two different fabrics, or ½ yard of one fabric.

JUST ONE QUILT block—the simple, endlessly useful half-square triangle block—is all it takes to make this beautiful and surprisingly easy star quilt. But the star quilt is just the beginning!

This chapter also includes eight completely different patterns you can make from this same set of sixteen triangle blocks. All you have to do to make one of the alternate designs is simply arrange the blocks as shown in one of the patterns on the following pages. Everything else about making the quilt is exactly the same–cutting, layering, quilting, and finishing.

The instructions for this project go briefly over techniques that are covered in detail in Chapters 5 and 6. Go back to those chapters if you need a refresher.

1. Choosing Fabrics for this Quilt

This pattern calls for two fabrics: one lighter and one darker. I chose white and a rose floral print for the quilt pictured on the left, with white for the middle and backing layers. The color possibilities are endless, though. You just need to make sure the fabrics you choose have enough contrast to show off the triangular shapes that make the star pattern.

2. Cut the Fabrics

Cut the following squares:

Top Layer

- Eight 12" squares of white fabric

- Eight 12" squares of floral fabric

Middle Layer

- Sixteen 12" squares

Bottom Layer

- Sixteen 12" squares

Edge Trim Strips

- Six 1-1/2" strips of each edge trim fabric, or 12 strips if you use only one fabric.

3. Make the Half-Square Triangle Blocks

This easy method for making half-square triangle blocks starts with fabric squares. Each set of two squares will make two mirror-image triangle blocks.

- Take the light squares you cut for the top layer of the quilt and stack them on your work surface with their right sides down. Use a ruler and a fine-point permanent marker to draw a diagonal line from corner to corner across the back of each square. The line won't show when the blocks are finished.

- Lay each light square together with a dark square, right sides together. Align the edges and corners carefully.

- Sew a seam 1/4" away from each side of the line you marked. (If you have a ¼" quilting foot, using it makes this easy.) The dotted red lines in the photo represent the lines to sew:

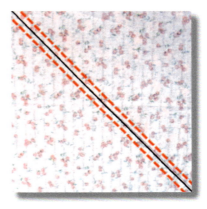

- Making this quilt involves piecing a whole set of sixteen triangle blocks at one time. You can speed up the sewing and save yourself some thread by chain piecing the blocks. Chain piecing means that as you reach the end of one block, you feed the next block under the presser foot and sew right onto it without cutting the thread between blocks. This is what a set of chain-pieced blocks looks like:

- After you have sewed all the blocks, use your rotary cutter or a pair of scissors to cut the thread between blocks.

- Use a ruler and rotary cutter to cut along the center line. You will get two triangular units that look like this:

- Open the blocks and press the seam allowance to the darker side. Press with an up-and-down movement of your iron to avoid stretching the diagonal lines of the block. Try not to push the fabric from side to side. You will end up with two mirror-image half-square triangle blocks:

- The completed blocks will have little tails at two of their corners. Use a ruler to square up the blocks and trim off the tails.

4. Layer the Blocks

The half-square triangle blocks you just made will be almost half an inch smaller than the original fabric squares you started with. If this were a conventional quilt, that would be enough to raise your blood pressure a few points. But this is a rag quilt, so it's no problem at all! Here's what to do:

- Lay a backing fabric square on your work surface, right side down.

- Lay a middle fabric square on top of the backing fabric, right side up. Align the corners and edges so they are straight.

- Lay one of the triangle blocks you just made on top of the other layers, right side up. Center the block so you can see an equal-sized rim of lower layers all around the outside of the block. When you sew the blocks together, you will end up with a little extra edge of lower layers in the seam allowances. After you clip the seams and wash the quilt, you won't even remember it's there.

- Quilt the blocks with any of the methods described in Chapter 5, or choose your own quilting pattern.

5. Lay Out and Sew the Blocks

- Lay the quilted blocks on your work surface so they are arranged the way you want them to look when the quilt is finished. Check your layout against the photograph of the quilt on page 32.

- It's easy to get disoriented when you're working with a lot of identical blocks. I always put a safety pin in the block on the top left corner to help me keep my bearings while I sew.

- Sew the blocks together, one row at a time. I sew each row from left to right, starting with the top row, then working my way down to the bottom of the quilt, one row at a time.

- Sew the rows together. Pin at seam lines to make sure the rows don't get out of alignment while you sew.

6. Add the Edge Trim Strips

Lay two layers of trim strips around the outer edges of the quilt and sew them on.

7. Clip the Seams and Edges

Using your rag snippers or spring-loaded scissors, clip all the seams between strips and all around the outside of the quilt. Clip both sides of the trim strips.

8. Wash and Dry the Quilt

Run the quilt through the wash and dryer to fluff up the clipped seams, wash off the basting spray, and get rid of lint and little clipped threads.

H ERE'S A TRIANGLE Star quilt I made with three fabrics instead of two. Isn't it interesting how different that extra fabric makes the quilt look?

Make Eight More Quilts with These Triangle Blocks

O**NE MAGICAL QUALITY** of the wonderful half-square triangle block is that you can make so many different quilts with it. Here are eight more quilt patterns you can make with the same sixteen blocks that go into the Triangle Star quilt. Each pattern is shown much larger on the following pages. To make one of these patterns, follow the cutting and sewing instructions from the Triangle Star quilt project, but use the alternate pattern as a guide for arranging your blocks. That's how easy it is!

Diamond in a Square

Fields and Furrows

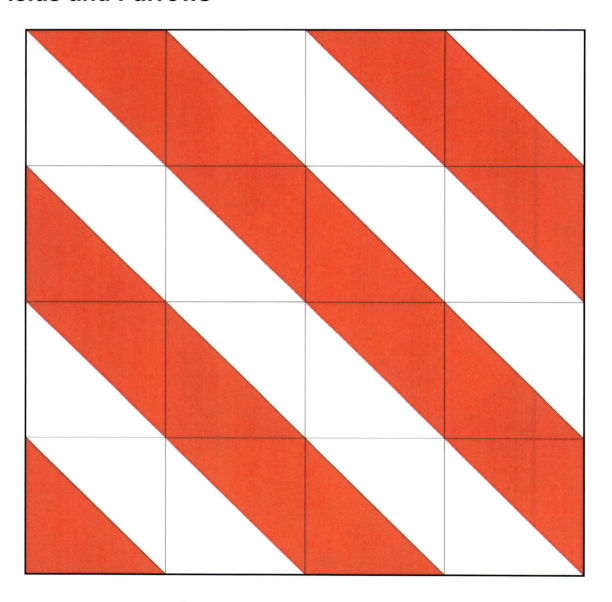

Hunter's Star

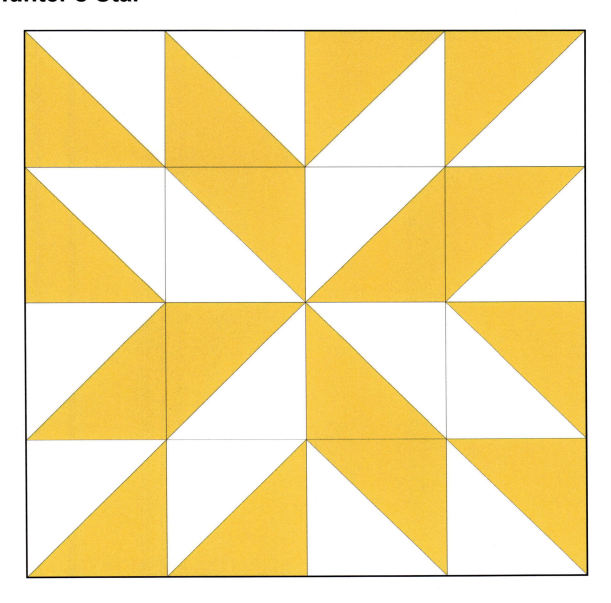

Pinwheels

Pueblo

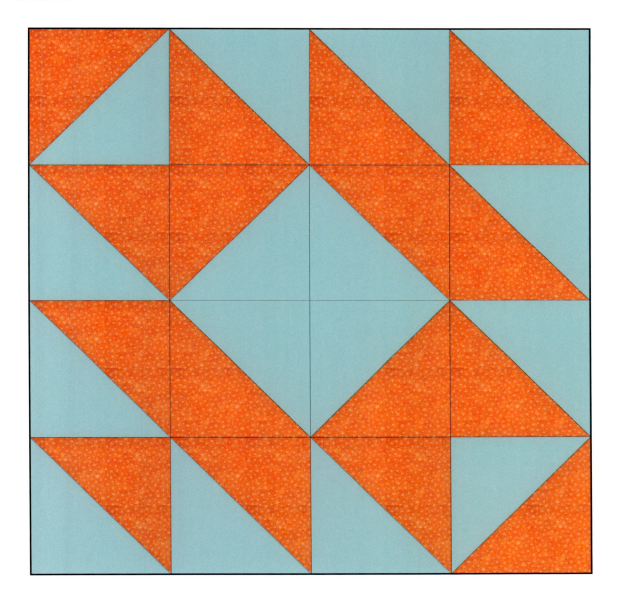

Straight Set Triangles

Tilted Diamonds

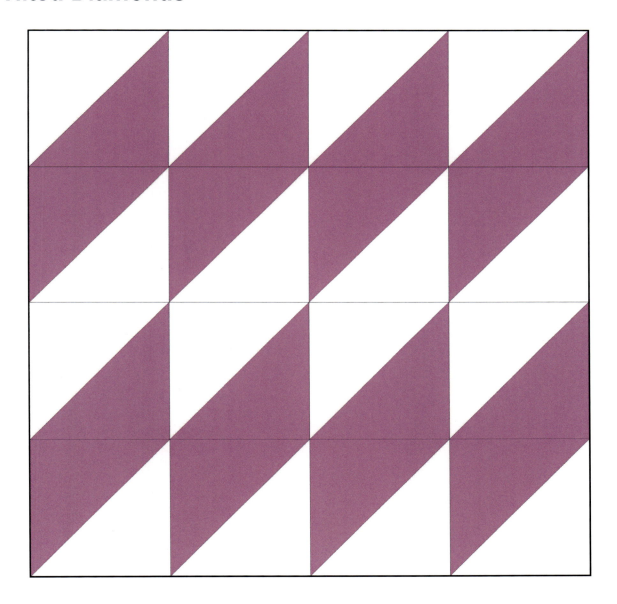

Zig Zag

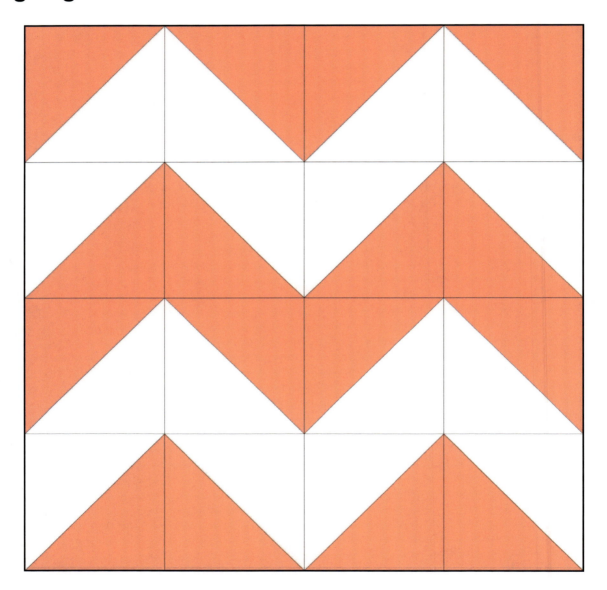

9/ More on Quilting from Felicity Walker

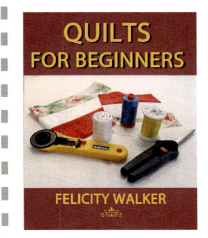

You can make a beautiful quilt from start to finish, and love doing it – even if you've never made a quilt in your life. Felicity's best-selling guide for new quilters shows you how to make a quilt step by step, with lots of photos and helpful tips to make learning fun and easy.

Everything you need to know is covered, from the tools and supplies you'll need, to choosing fabrics, cutting, piecing, basting and layering, machine quilting, and binding. Includes three easy patterns with complete instructions to get you started. Join the thousands of other quilters who have gotten their start with help from *Quilts for Beginners*. Available in paperback or as an e-book. Find out why this book has 40 five-star reviews on Amazon.com: grab a free sample chapter at http://amzn.to/1zQ4pe6.

About Felicity

I have been quilting for nearly 20 years and have made hundreds of quilts, but I still think of myself as a beginning quilter. I was surprised and deeply gratified by the popularity of my first book for new quilters. It's my goal to help you and other quilters find fast, fun, and easy ways to enjoy the art of making things with fabric.

If you have any questions after reading this book, or if there is any way I can help you enjoy quilting more, please do email me for more information. I love to hear from readers. You can reach me at info@quiltersdiary.com.

If you find that this book has helped you, I ask you to please leave a review for others so they can get started quilting too. To post a review, just visit the *Rag Quilting for Beginners* page on Amazon.com and scroll down until you reach the button that says "Write a customer review." Click the button to add your review.

Felicity Walker

Photo Credits

All photos in this book were taken by Felicity Walker, except those credited below, which are used with permission under a Creative Commons license:

Page Number	Photo Credit
3	Sweet Baby Jamie, Flickr. https://flic.kr/p/7VnvAz
7	Quilt with gray sashing, Gabrielle, Flickr. https://flic.kr/p/9wxtyb
7	Denim rag quilt, Kim, Flickr. https://flic.kr/p/gdwtU9
7	Quilt binding detail, Gina Pina, Flickr. https://flic.kr/p/9fpSN2
7	Rag quilt with shirt fabric, Renee, Flickr. https://flic.kr/p/ndc3K
11	Cat in quilt, Joel Dinda, Flickr. https://flic.kr/p/be3tsD
12	Blue and gray quilt, Martha Merry, Flickr. https://flic.kr/p/d6pLMy
18	Unclipped quilt, cyndygysbers, Flickr. https://flic.kr/p/aWkeCt
21	Cottage chic rag quilt detail, Martha Merry, Flickr. https://flic.kr/p/d6pLMy
23	Rag quilt on bench, Lynn Gardner, Flickr. https://flic.kr/p/dbqZom

Made in the USA
Columbia, SC
27 February 2019